McKinnon ♡ 2-22-'—

I can't tell you enough,
how proud I am of you.
Your a very special Young
Man & I'am so greatful
to be your Grandma. ○.

Dear Grandson

Life Lessons from Your Grandmother

Written by **Judy Smith**

Photography by **Lou Guarracino**

Dear Grandson,

Being your grandmother is one of the greatest joys of my life. You have instilled a newness into my life, a warmth into my soul and a brighter song in my heart. As your grandmother, I take this as my responsibility to guide you on your precious path through life. I hope to instill in you pieces of the wisdom I have gained throughout my own journey.

My wish is for you to become the kind of man that speaks his mind yet appropriately holds his tongue when needed. Someone who is strong minded and gentle souled, spirited and spiritual, loving and lovable.

It is my honor to be your grandmother and I shall be forever grateful for having you in my life.

Adoringly,
Your Grandmother

A Mate For Your Soul

Your Grandmother might not be your ideal source for obtaining advice on love, however as someone who has loved and lost, I have learned what love is and what love is not.

In my eyes, no one will ever be good enough for you. However make sure to find someone who is good for your soul and is someone who will embrace your vision and not try to change it. Fall in love with someone who does the right things, not someone who says the right things.

Falling in Love

- Love her unconditionally and put her above all others.
- Listen to her with sincerity.
- Have an interest in her life, her likes and dislikes.
- Hold her hand, often.
- Compliment her.
- Wait for the right woman to come along...she's out there.

Appreciate Yourself

Your happiness and self-worth are not dependent on what others may think of you. Believe in yourself first and the rest will come. Make the conscious decision to have faith in yourself and abilities. The moment you begin to believe in yourself, things will change rapidly.

Art of Acceptance

Accepting a difficult situation as it is does not mean you agree with it, only that you understand you are not able to change it. You can only change how you allow it to affect you.

Keep going, the most difficult roads to maneuver lead to the best destinations.

Art of Nothingness

If I could teach you just
one thing, it would be
the art of stillness. Calm
your mind and allow the
gift of nature's bounty
to surround you with
peace. Find the beauty of
everyday things: clouds,
birds, music, water,
trees...

Be Curious

Find the deeper meaning in things, discover the hidden personality
traits of your friends and family, question and seek understanding with
your interests. Be open to new opportunities.

Be a Gentle Man

There's no excuse for
leaving the house with
un-brushed teeth, nails
untrimmed or hair unkempt.
It's ok to be scruffy — just
be controlled scruffy!

- *If it is cold outside, offer a lady your jacket.*
- *Do not touch your food until all the ladies at your table have been served.*
- *Avoid profane language in front of all females.*
- *When walking down the street with a lady, walk on the street side.*
- *Look a girl directly into her eyes, never at her body; you will see more beauty.*
- *Listen…intently to what she has to say.*
- *Open and hold the door for all ladies. Make this your calling card.*

Being at ease with who you are is the sign of a true gentleman.
Being a gentleman never goes out of style and is always noticed!

Be Playful

Never forget what it was like to be a child. Jump, skip, laugh, and embrace fun things in life, no matter how frivolous. When the daily grind becomes overwhelming, go into play mode and things will start to change and your stress level will go down.

Growing older doesn't mean we stop playing. Continue to play to avoid growing old.

Be in the Moment

Focus on one task at a time rather than trying to accomplish everything at once.

When thinking of nothing, you ultimately feel everything. When thinking of everything, you feel nothing.

Change Your Attitude

Alter the way you view things and the things you are viewing will be altered. Changing your attitude is always the quickest route to changing your life.

We Are All Unique

Don't compare your life with others. You have no idea
what their journey is about. This can lead you to overlook
what is truly unique about you. Celebrate you!

Count Your Blessings

- Count your blessings, instead of your losses.
- Every day reflect on three things for which you are grateful.
- Say thank you to the people in your life—often!
- The best is yet to be! At all times, some of the best days of your life are ahead.

Enjoy the Journey

Goals are important but not at the expense of your happiness.
Maintain a balance between getting to where you want to go
and being happy as you get there.

Follow Your Own Path

There will be others with
you on your path through
life, guiding and comforting
you. However, the lesson
you learn on your travels is
truly yours alone.

Forgive and You Will Heal

You will be hurt and you will be disappointed. While you can't control the deeds of others, you have total control over what you allow the actions of others to do to you. Forgiveness will release the heavy burden of carrying around the pain and suffering in your own heart.

With forgiveness, we become unwilling to wish harm to another. By seeing how a painful situation has helped you grow, you will find peace and serenity. Forgiveness builds character that we would not have known without the initial hurt.

Friendship

Surround yourself with others who value and
appreciate you. All you need are a few "real" people in
your life who truly understand and love you.

Generosity

Give more to others than they expect and do so willingly.

Getting Off the Couch

Move, dance, play, run, skip and soar.

Give Without Expectations

Wrap up your inner self in a bright package and give it to others. Give
of your talents, your laughter, your affection, encouragement and love.
Do not expect or require anything in return…it comes back to you.

Gratitude

Be thankful for what you have — health, family, shelter, food.

Be thankful for what you don't have — illness, loneliness, homelessness.

Have Order in Your Life

Order welcomes calmness in your life which precedes clear thought. This allows room in our lives for happiness and success.

Have You Read Any Good Books Lately?

Not only is reading a mind expanding exercise, it also removes us from
our daily lives. Search for new hobbies, expand your visions
and let your mind grow. Read often—it's magical!

Must Reads:

- *Don Quixote* by Miguel de Cervantes
- *Moby Dick* by Herman Melville
- *The Great Gatsby* by F. Scott Fitzgerald
- *The Prince* by Niccolo Machiavelli
- *Catcher in the Rye* by J.D. Salinger
- *How to Cook Everything* by Mark Bittman
- *Catch 22* by Joseph Heller
- *Lord of the Rings* by J.R.R. Tolkien
- *Walden* by Henry David Thoreau
- *Secrets of Closing the Sale* by Zig Ziglar
- *How to Win Friends and Influence People* by Dale Carnegie
- *1984* by George Orwell
- *A Young Man's Guide* by William Alcott
- *The Sun Also Rises* by Ernest Hemingway
- *Siddhartha* by Hermann Hesse
- *To Kill a Mockingbird* by Harper Lee
- *The Grapes of Wrath* by John Steinbeck

I Have Learned...

- We truly get treated the way we treat others.

- Respect and love yourself and others will do the same.

- Everyone deserves a second chance.

- I do not seek perfection. I seek to be honest and true to myself…flaws and all.

- To accept what I have, be happy with what I have, who I am and where I am.

- To be thankful for what you have and you will always be rewarded with more.

- Motivation comes in short spurts, grab it while it's hot.

Learning From Criticism

Do not ignore harsh criticism, it will help you
grow and develop. Respond in a calm and
positive manner and remove emotions from
the equation. Do not allow your sense of ego
to stand in the way of objectively reviewing the
comments. This will open the door to accept
constructive criticism and ultimately improve the
quality of your life.

Live Simply

Practice the art of living simply by having things in your home and office arranged in a way that will relax and energize you.

Fortify Your Soul

- *Make wise choices in your diet.*

- *Exercise often.*

- *Sleep on the same schedule as much as possible.*

Live the Lifestyle

Having money is not the key to happiness, however it does provide the self-sufficiency needed to give you the freedom to share yourself creatively and freely without worries of finances.

Always remember:

- *What you save is more important than what you earn.*

- *Share your good fortune with others when they need it.*

- *Respect the things you have and avoid waste.*

- *Mentally live the lifestyle you desire.*

Networking

Stay in touch with people you respect. Welcome opportunities, personally and professionally.

Peacefulness

It is easy to allow lifes challenges to disturb your tranquility. Life is far too precious to be wasted on nonessential issues. Find the balance. Be kind, but don't be abused. Trust, but avoid deception. Be content, but continue to improve yourself.

Perfect Imperfections

Ignore the flaws in people and things. You will be amazed at the hidden perfections.

Put the Electronics Down

There is an entire universe looming out there woven together by sun, clouds, mountains and valleys.

Pursue the Right Career

Be passionate about your job and choose a career that will fulfill a passion and bring you happiness. When we follow our authentic path, we are using gifts that have been bestowed upon us. By seeking wonder, the money and success will follow.

Do what you love but also learn to love what you do.

Rejoice in Your Individuality

No one else is exactly like you.

Truth be Told

Always be true to yourself and you will never feel the need to be false to others.

Sounds of Silence

Laying deep in your soul, tucked away from all of lifes interruptions, is golden silence leading to your dreams. There lie your passions, your secrets, your bliss. Try and find that place every day with just a few moments of silence. Listen to what the stillness is saying to you.

Try Something New... Often

Growth comes when we step out of our comfort zone.

Sometimes You Win, Sometimes You Lose

Win without acting like it's the first time you have won at anything. Lose without losing control.

Welcome a New Day!

Enjoy the early morning hours with peace, quiet and reflection by taking a few minutes to simply breathe. The most glorious part of the day is the sunrise when the day slowly gets brighter, when the dark blue sky turns a lighter hue and the brilliant colors seep into the sky. Breathe in the glory of a new day.

What Would you Do
if you Knew you Could not Fail?

Imagine not having the fear to do the things you want to do in life. Today, at this very moment, you have the ability, wisdom, and strength to be all you want to be and have all your dreams come true. Trust in yourself, toss the fears aside and let the hues of your bright future shine through.

Your greatest success will come as a result of a previous failure.

Participate in life- never withdraw.

Never give up…this is not an option.

Your Grandmother will always be your biggest cheerleader!

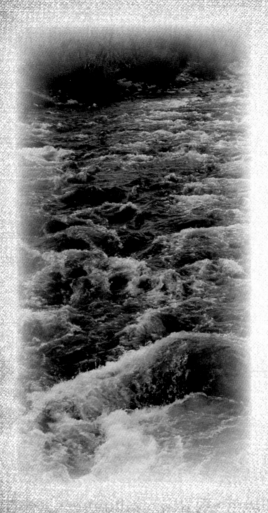

Life is a Struggle

It is designed to challenge
your abilities and strengthen
your problem solving skills.
Growth does not come when
life is easy, it comes when the
struggles are the hardest. Life
can be hard but you, my dear
grandson, have what it takes
to tackle it.